Creating Fame Online

Small Business Marketing Secrets That Will Attract More Clients & Explode Your Sales

Heatherr Jumah

Creating Fame Online

Foreword

Creating Fame Online is an important book for any small business owner to read. Those of us who are veterans of Internet marketing know successful online business promotion never happens just by building a site and hoping customers will find it. Developing a successful website for your business is not rocket science – but expertise does involve a pretty steep learning curve. That's why I like this book so much. It gives business owners an intelligent overview of what it takes to thrive online. The result is the potential for widespread economic recovery starting at the small business level.

This book presents local online marketing in a way that even the most tech-adverse business owner can get an understanding of what they need to do next. It highlights some of the challenges in today's marketing world, and gives practical advice on overcoming them. It shows companies how to connect better, faster, and easier with their prospective customers using the Internet.

If you own a business, this book was written for you. In these pages you'll find hope – hope that your business can thrive even today, hope that you might be able to get back to whatever it was that attracted you to your field in the first place rather than working all the time to try to get new customers. Most importantly it provides a process for helping you connect with the people who really need the products and services your business offers.

Heatherr explains local Internet marketing in a simple, conversational style that makes for an easy read. That's not to say any of this complicated strategy was over-simplified. In fact, I'm proud to see how well the discussion matches with my extensive, industry-leading course on the subject.

Anyone wanting to double or triple their business should read and re-read this book. It can literally turn a dying business into one that's booming again. Around my company's headquarters, we often say we're in the business of creating heroes. Thanks, Heatherr. Through your book, you're making a difference.

Mike Koenigs

Table of Contents

Yippee

Yippee. You've got your own business, or practice, or whatever you want to call it. It's all yours (well, and the bank's or whoever you've got calling or mailing you on a regular basis asking for payments). And how wonderful that you've achieved your childhood dream of getting paid to do always and only what you LOVE to do.

OK. So maybe not.

In fact, if you could travel back in time to meet with your young self, all bright-eyed and enthusiastic about this endeavor, you might smack yourself silly for thinking that THING you wanted to do would be just about all you'd have to do in order to have a successful business.

That younger version of you - hair intact and fully pigmented - never dreamed of all the OTHER stuff you'd find yourself doing day in and day out. The planning, the marketing, the sales, the scheduling, the re-scheduling, the supply ordering (how is it you go through so many pens, and where do they GO?), the accounts payable, the accounts receivable, the never-ending cycle of hiring, training, firing, and replacing, payroll, bookkeeping, researching, buying, learning, and maintaining all your equipment... exhausted yet?

Oh yes, and there's that THING you wanted to do. The thing that started all of this. You probably went to school a while for this. Probably took on some debt. Probably invested some money and time and sweat to learn how to do it well. At one point you loved this thing - maybe you still do. But it sure seems like a lot of trouble having to do all that other stuff so you get to do that thing.

It gets worse.

Just a few years ago, there was this big, thick book published every year that magically put some money into your coffers. Customers, patients, clients - whatever you call them in your world - opened this book, found your business, called, and then spent money with you. The phone book... sure it cost you an arm and a leg, but the ads worked (for the most part, sort of). Sure you grew to hate the sight of your rep, your wallet sweating every year when they came to renew your ad, always with the pressure to try something bigger, bolder, more colorful. But at least it sort of worked.

Now, not so much. Unless your customers fit certain die-hard phone book user demographics. Otherwise, your customers probably can't remember where they shoved their phone book. Or it went right into recycling as soon as it was delivered. Or if you're in a metropolitan area, it was one of several different books they received - and they chose to keep the one you decided not to advertise in this year.

The marketing spaghetti toss - you know, throw a bunch of stuff at the wall and see what sticks - it's expensive, head-bangingly frustrating, and more than a little scary. You know you've got to have a steady stream of feet through your door, butts in your seats, or however else you measure profitability. Not only do you have to get these people to come in once, in most businesses, you've got to keep them coming back. You know it's not cutting it just being a business networking group member, joining a leads swapping group, or advertising every-where you can think of.

You know the Internet's inevitable for you. You probably even have a website. Possibly even a really great-looking one. And if it's not so great-looking (thanks to your brother's idiot nephew who swore he could build you one that would be 'awesome', you've probably got plans and dreams for the site you'd really like to have. Maybe you've got website envy - your competitor's got the site you'd love to have someday. You keep hearing how important it is to get your business online, to build an Internet presence, to use social media to get new customers, to tap into the power of the web...

Sure. You need one more (huge) challenge for your business. In your spare time. Oh yes, and one with a pretty steep learning curve.

"Got a sharp stick I could poke my eyes out with?" Yeah, I know.

That's why I'm giving you this book.

That THING you do in your business? Well, my thing is marketing businesses like yours. I like it. I'm good at it. I've invested time, money, and sweat learning what works, what doesn't work so well, and what's going to work best for your kind of business. Whatever it is that you do as your THING, it's not something I can do for myself, probably -

and for sure it wouldn't be the best use of my time and energy learning how to do it, or trying to do it. But I bet if you had a book on it that broke all the steps and processes into manageable bites and translated all the jargon into plain English, I could learn enough about it to understand what I needed to learn more about in order to do it, or to learn that no way, no how did I want to have to do that thing for myself, ever.

This is that book.

One way you'll benefit by giving it a quick read is that there are a lot of people out there who would love nothing better than to take your money and not do squat for you, and hopefully this will help you avoid them. Or, maybe you actually DO want to do all your own marketing for your business, and this will help you understand what you'd need to do to make it work. Maybe you're starting from square one as far as online marketing goes; this should help you avoid some costly pitfalls and develop a battle plan before you start throwing money around.

Or, maybe you've got a site that's sucking your money into a black abyss, your website developer has disappeared, the site's outdated, unattractive, and just sitting there - and you'd rather stick your finger in a socket than deal with trying to fix it.

This should help.

Cheer up; it won't be so bad. In fact, this could be a major turning point in your business. Learning just a little bit about this - enough to take some action - could mean the difference between closing your doors (or wishing you could) and expansion. The info you're about to read has helped many, many businesses double, triple, or grow even more than that, even in a challenged economy.

If your competitors have been stealing your lunch money lately when it comes to getting new customers, that's about to stop. Your phone book ad rep would break a sweat seeing you read this, because the next call you'd make might be to be sure your ad doesn't renew because you'll be "going another direction" next time.

You might even put this book down in a couple of hours feeling more optimistic than you've felt in a long, long time. You'll understand some stuff you've never really had anyone explain clearly before, your brain will begin hatching all kinds of new ideas, and you'll see the start of a game plan you can actually follow to restore some sanity to your life.

This Means War

Nobody should ever start anything without some sort of plan in place. Doesn't have to be completely fleshed out to the nth degree with every contingency accounted for - but it's awfully hard to hit an undefined target. You need a battle plan. At stake, the future profitability and (dare we even say this?) enjoyment of running your business.

What's the end goal? More, better customers (clients, patients - we'll just go with customers to keep it simple). Meaning, you've got all the customers you want, anytime you want them - and they're paying you well and walking away happy. Not asking much, huh?

Think about this from the customer's side. Think about a favorite business you frequent (or one you remember from being a kid - since everything looks rosier with a couple of decades in the rear-view mirror). This business was THE best at something. You looked forward to going there, you told your friends about it, you told people you didn't even know about it, you knew without a doubt that THIS was the place to go for (fill in the blank). You didn't even really mind if they raised prices - and you weren't alone, because the place pretty much had a line wrapped around the building anytime the doors were open.

Now, maybe this business WAS the best... but maybe, just maybe, it benefited just a tiny bit from peoples' perception being contagious. It was seen as the best because it was seen as the best. Nothing wrong with that - and certainly a dog of a business would have a hard time convincing anyone it's the best - but it makes the 'best' status a little more attainable. Also good news because it means your business doesn't truly have to be the hands-down winner of measurable 'best-ness' in order to enjoy outrageous success.

One of your primary goals in marketing is to become known as the go-to business for whatever it is you offer. There's a sense of expertise involved. Probably this isn't an issue for you, but if you do happen to feel a little overwhelmed by the 'expert' label, consider that an expert really only needs to know more than, say, 90% of people out there in the general population. If you've been in business for any length of time, it's pretty safe to assume you're an expert in your field.

Why is this important?

People want to do business with people they know, like, and trust. They want to business with an expert because time's short, resources can be tight, and frankly, they just don't want to mess around doing business with a hack.

Generally, people will give some benefit of the doubt that you're an expert - just by virtue of the fact that you're in business. But there's a lot you can do to help that perception along. It's not bragging or boasting - it's actually a matter of helping your prospective customers get what they want and need.

How does this play out in your online marketing?

This is huge - and it's the foundation of everything you need to do online for your business. You want it to be that anytime someone goes looking online for the products or services you offer, there you are. You want it so that everywhere they turn online, they find information, positive reviews, maps, directory listings, news, articles, videos, and more - all pointing to YOU as the go-to resource they've been looking for. If you do enough to promote your business (and give value even to people who aren't yet your customers), you will achieve online domination. You will become practically untouchable by your competitors.

OK, so let's get to work. Let me give you an overall understanding of how this all plays out online.

Let's say you sit down at your computer and go looking for... information on how to train your dog.

- Chances are, you'll use Google (it's by far the most-used search engine, dwarfing all the others by a mile) - but maybe you'll use Bing or Yahoo.
- You type in: how to train a dog (or something similar). This is called a keyword (or keyword phrase).
- You get a list of results (websites, articles, blog posts, videos, products, maybe even a trainer or two).

At the top of that list you'll probably have a few 'sponsored' results - these are ads. They're at the top of the list because someone paid for them to be there. The moment that advertiser stops paying for the ad, it disappears. Same thing with many searches where you get sponsored results to the right of the screen.

As an aside, these ads are created through a program called AdWords. It's a Pay Per Click (PPC) advertising model - you bid on ad space according to the words you choose, and you only pay up to your bid amount anytime someone clicks your ad. Unless you've got experience running a PPC campaign, or you have unlimited marketing funds, you may not want to go that route on your own - you can run up a huge tab pretty quickly and not get much in the way of results.

Anyway, once you scroll down past the ads, you get to what's called organic results. There are ten of these per page in most cases. These are websites, articles, blog posts, videos, etc. that Google has determined to be relevant to what you went looking for.

This is important. Relevancy is very important to Google. Here's why... if you went looking for tips on training your dog and ended up with a list of results that ranged from oatmeal cookie recipes to hot vacation destinations to how to sharpen a pencil - well, you'd probably never use Google again. And that would mean Google lost (usership, revenue, and respect) - and the one rule to get straight right off the bat is that Google never loses. So, Google strives to make absolutely sure that no matter what, the results it comes up with are relevant to what the user hoped to find.

With that in mind, when someone goes looking online for the products or services you sell, Google WANTS to include your business in those search results.

Trouble is, Google's pretty clever - but it doesn't know everything. And unless you've made an effort for Google to know your business, it's not going to bet the farm in speculating what you do.

Back to our example. You've got a dog that needs training. You're looking at about 3.7 million results that Google suggested for you. Alright - now it's time to read all of them.

No?

Of course not. In fact, you probably will stop clicking after the first page. Certainly after the first few - and you'd have to have one bad dog to keep reading up to that point. Most online searchers end with the first page. In fact, most end with the first few organic results - the ones that appear "above the fold". Above the fold is a reference to print news-papers - the front top of the first page has all the stories most likely to cause someone to plunk down a few coins to buy the paper. Online, above the fold is what you can see without scrolling down.

Those top several results on the first page of Google are statistically far more likely to get clicked than others toward the bottom.

Not to jump ahead too far, but YOU WANT THOSE TOP SPOTS! In fact, you want as many spots as you can get, as high as you can get them. (So does your competitor.)

Nobody knows exactly how Google determines what's going to appear in those top spots. If you ever hear an Internet marketer complaining about Google changing its algorithm, that's what that is - some mysterious calculation they use to see how to order the results.

While we don't know all the details, we have figured out how to make Google like a website enough to list it toward the top. We know what Google likes, and what Google hates.

Quick aside here - one thing Google hates is being tricked. There's a whole industry out there called "Black Hat SEO" - it's sneaky, bad guy kind of stuff with the whole goal of making Google like a website under false pretenses. The tactics are constantly evolving, but the end result is always the same - eventually Google figures out what the black hatter did and bans websites that are using this sneaky stuff.

So, how do you make Google like your site?

You play fair. You offer real, valuable content. You don't try to play games.

It's a bit like a popularity contest, really. Someone searches on Google, and Google scours the Internet looking for the most relevant results possible. It looks at your website (if you're catching Google's attention) to evaluate whether your site is a relevant results. It looks at other websites to see whether they've got an opinion of your site's relevance for that search. It pays special attention to websites it already respects. The goal is to have all of these (your site and other respected sites) essentially voting for your website.

And the best news is, you can stuff the ballot box. That means your website will get listed toward the top, you'll make it easier for more prospective customers to find you online (even if they don't know your name), they'll visit your site and be far more likely to call or come in, and they'll want to do business with you.

The rest of this book is going to lay out a plan for you to achieve online domination. It's a bit like playing chess - but with the end goal of helping your customers to get what they really want and need (you!).

The Secret Sauce

Know how in most projects, there's a preparation phase that's boring, tricky, tedious, and yet completely crucial to the success of the rest of the project?

That's this part.

Skip this, and you'll be in good (bad?) company. You'll get to dive into dozens of online marketing tasks that are way more fun - but you won't be able to do them correctly. You'll jump ahead to the part where you get to climb the ladder - but you'll figure out pretty quickly your ladder wasn't leaning on the right tree.

What is it? Keyword research.

Yes, just as boring and techy as it sounds. But without it, you'll completely waste your time and money and get way less than optimal results.

We'll try to make this as painless as possible.

What Is Keyword Research?

When people go searching for information, products, and services, what they type into Google (and we'll just use Google to represent all of the search engines) is a keyword. A keyword could actually be a whole phrase - even a really long one - or just a single word.

Keyword research involves studying how people search online. Seems like it would be pretty intuitive and straight-forward, until you dig a little deeper. For our example of searching for dog training tips, keyword research might reveal that people go looking for that same information using these key-words:

- how to train a dog
- dog training
- tips for training dogs
- how can I get my dog to stop barking?
- dog barks
- puppy training
- Labrador Retriever training

- my dog won't stop barking at the delivery man
- dog bark help
- why does my dog bark
- puppies help
- help dogs
- …and about a million other variations

People search in odd ways online. Sometimes in ways you'd never imagine. Sometimes with misspellings, 'wrong' terms, slang, bad grammar, and generalities or specifics that are mind-boggling.

It's just about impossible to predict how your customers will go looking for you online. It's really better not to even try, because you'll always be wrong - you just may not know it.

There are four major traps you can fall into with keyword research:

Mistake #1: Skip it altogether.
We've already gone over why that's a really, really bad idea.

Mistake #2: Look at your neighbor's paper.
You can tell from the wording that this will be a mistake - and for some of the same reasons this isn't a good idea in school, either. It happens, though. A business owner

decides it's time to get busy online and hears something about keywords being important. They go to their competitor's website and do some poking around to discover what keywords that guy's going after. That guy seems smart enough, so the keywords are probably good.

Trouble is, you don't know how he got his keywords or whether they're performing well. You're going to be spending a lot of time trying to get Google to associate these keywords with your website; it would be a shame to chase after keywords that stink. Worse yet, you'll be competing with that guy for these keywords - and if they stink, it's an even bigger loss.

Mistake #3: Forget to actually use them.

Sounds crazy, but even after compiling a list of great key-words, some people just file the list away and forget to actually use what they've learned. It's like custom-crafting fine marble tiles and then using a cheap laminate for your kitchen instead. You'll want to refer to your list of great keywords constantly as you work on marketing your site.

Mistake #4: Only do your keyword research once.

Doing keyword research the right way is an ongoing process. It's not something you can do just once and then cross it off of your to-do list forever. There are a couple of reasons for this.

Chances are, your business is multi-faceted and there are multiple ways people might go looking for your products and services online. There are multiple angles you could pursue as far as your keywords go, and it's unlikely you will be able to go after all of them exhaustively in one attempt.

For example, consider a dental practice that's looking to use the Internet to get more patients. Depending on what sort of specialties the dentist has, it might work to go after pain-free dental treatment, pediatric dental, restorative or cosmetic dental services, or even sedation dentistry. There are hundreds of keywords that could work for each of these niches. Doing exhaustive research on each of them could take weeks.

Rather than trying to get all of your keyword research done at one time, it's a better idea to do thorough research on one particular part of your business and then come back and add another part later. Otherwise, you may never get past the research stage, which is useless on its own.

Another reason you'll need to revisit your keyword research is changes in your industry or individual business. Again, for dentists, if you get advanced training on a new procedure and want to market your new service online, you'll need to know how people are searching for that procedure. The same holds true if you get new equipment, a new product line, or some sort of new technology that people are looking for. As conditions and offerings change in your business, you'll want to be sure your online presence connects with the changing way prospective customers look for you.

So, how do you do keyword research?

There are a number of ways to perform this task - none of which are particularly quick and easy, but there are a few that aren't too complicated. Be prepared to spend several hours doing your keyword research. It's not a process that can be hurried, and it's important enough that it's worth taking the time to do it correctly.

Keyword research tool options include some that you pay for (either a one-time fee or a pay-as-you-go option), and some that are free. Some are fairly easy to use, and some have such a steep learning curve that they're really not appropriate for non-Internet marketing professionals' use. For the best possible keyword research results, you may want to outsource this task to an expert. They typically have access to sophisticated keyword research tools and know how to use them efficiently. Purchasing the better tools and learning how to use them is probably not the best use of your time - and because you'll want to do your keyword research a bit at a time, you'll end up spending a considerable amount of time trying to remember how to use the tools.

That said, two keyword research tools you should consider are:

Google's External Keyword Tool
This tool is free, and offered by Google. It's connected to the Ad-Words advertising program, but doesn't require you to run ads in order to use it. The research results you'll get all come from the perspective of how your keywords will compete with paid advertisers on Google's various ad networks.

You can do your research with this tool two different ways. One is by entering 'seed' or starter keywords into the search field; the other is by entering your existing website into the website field and allowing Google to guess what your site is about. Obviously if you're just starting to work on your site, or if it hasn't been optimized for keywords (a good likelihood for most businesses) Google may have a hard time coming up with good keyword suggestions just by analyzing your site.

By entering some seed keywords into the tool, you can get keyword suggestions Google deems relevant in relation to those words. Some of them may surprise you. Some may be misspelled (your searchers don't always know how to spell your services, and sometimes they search without typing carefully). Some may include an 'incorrect' term (again, your searchers may not appreciate the subtleties of the semantics and jargon in your industry). They may also include search terms that are way more specific - or vague - than you would anticipate. For example, a search for air conditioning repair may actually come up as someone looking for a specific manufacturer's part number. Google's suggestions are generally pretty good - but you may find some that are completely off-topic.

The primary information you'll be able to gather from this tool is how many people searched for various keywords within the past month. There are tutorials on YouTube and in Google itself that will help you learn how to gather and interpret keyword data. There are ways you can do your research that will yield more or less valuable information.

Because the tool is intended for advertisers, you'll see some metrics that reference how competitive different keywords are based on how much advertisers are paying for their ads to show up for those keywords.

Market Samurai
This is a paid keyword research tool that won't break the bank. It's far more robust, providing not only keyword

suggestions, but multiple filters you can use to make sure the suggestions you get are as applicable as possible. It uses Google's data for some of its reports.

In addition to keyword suggestions and search volume statistics, this tool makes it easy to identify your top ten online competitors for any particular keyword. You'll be able to gather some valuable information about their online marketing efforts and what it will take to surpass them for your best keywords.

You can also track your website's progress in domination for different keywords. This means you can see at a glance how well your site is ranking on the three major search engines (Google, Bing, and Yahoo) for your keywords. You'll see what page your site is showing up on, whether you're gaining or losing ground, how many pages on your site are being indexed (meaning the search engine has noticed that page and is checking back periodically to see whether anything's changed on that page), and how many backlinks (we'll get into that later) point toward your website.

There are many other functions and features in Market Samurai, and the publisher offers dozens of video tutorials that make learning this software possible. You'll also find tutorials on YouTube which may be helpful.

Whatever tool you choose to do your keyword research, be prepared to spend several hours learning how to use the tool, then several more doing your research. It's not a fun task, but investing the time and effort needed to do it right will pay off.

What's a Good Keyword?

Different marketers qualify 'good' keywords differently - depending on the niche and the geographical area. In general, though, you want to find keywords that are low hanging fruit. You want a good balance between high search volume and low competition. The hard numbers for each of these metrics will vary wildly.

For example, keywords connected to the legal profession tend to be much more competitive than those in, say, environmental health and safety - and these same keywords will be harder to compete on in a metropolitan area than in a less populated area.

 As you do your research and analysis, you will find a sweet spot that has relatively high search volume and relatively low competition. Once you find words like that, focus on them and look for more with similar or better metrics.

If you aim for keywords that are too competitive, it will take much longer to make progress as far as your Google placement. You'll be in competition with businesses that may have been going for those keywords for years, businesses that may have much deeper pockets or a dedicated Internet marketing department. If you aim for key-words that are "too easy" they most likely won't have enough search volume to make your efforts pay off.

Here's the perfect example...

Sometimes business owners think they're doing really well with Google if when they type their own name or their business' name into Google's search box, their website comes up on the first page.

Get that?

The keyword they typed in was either their name or the name of their business. By all means, their site ought to come up toward the top of that list - or even better, take up most of the page of results!

However, that's not good enough. That only means someone who already knows you or your business can find you online. Essentially that equates to having an online business card.

What we're looking to do is very different.

We want to make sure that when people go looking for the products and services you offer - without even knowing your name or your business name - they find you. The keywords in this case are your products or services and most likely your geographical location.

It's pretty easy to rank for your name or your business name. Ranking well for your products and services is another matter. That's where online marketing pays off and delivers a high return on every advertising dollar.

Once you find that sweet spot for your keywords - high search volume and low competition, save those keywords to a spreadsheet. If you're using Market Samurai, you can just export your results to a spreadsheet. If you're using Google's tool, you can export the results to a spreadsheet - they just won't include as much information, so you'll have to go through more steps and some guesswork to get an idea of how well you can compete for those keywords.

Sort your keyword target list by priority, so you know which keywords you'll go after first. It's a good idea to even color code your list so you can get extreme clarity on which words are the priority. You might choose to focus on 5-10 keywords at a time, moving down your list after you've made solid progress on the first batch of keywords.

In the next chapter, we'll start looking at what you'll need to do with the keywords you've identified as winners for your business.

Getting Your Site
Ready for Company

Acronym time. The big one you need to know for your own
website is SEO - Search Engine Optimization. This
chapter's going to address what you need to do SEO-wise
on your website.

What Is SEO?

SEO means making your website attractive to the search
engines, making it clear to Google that your site is relevant
to your topic or industry. Every element of your website
will either appeal to or repel Google.

A good way to think about Google is kind of like a stray cat
- but one you want around. If you put out 'food' Google

likes, it'll keep coming back. If you set up an online environment (on your site) that boosts Google's confidence in your site, it'll keep coming back - and it'll send people your way. If you try tricking, teasing, taunting, or otherwise mistreating Google, it will bite you - hard.

Like it or not, today's online environment is ruled by Google.

So, what makes for a good website? One that Google loves? Again, we don't know with certainty what's on the checklist - but there are certain elements that are a sure thing. The guiding principle is that Google doesn't want to recommend a site to a searcher, have the searcher click to get to that site, and then bounce (clicking to another site immediately because that site wasn't at all what the searcher wanted to find). Google likes sites where searchers stick, or stay and visit several pages on the site, digging deeper and finding all kinds of relevant information.

Remember, your primary goal with your website is to build your credibility online. Your site visitors need to leave your site believing in your expertise.

A little aside here...

Following along with the stray cat analogy, Google's constantly on the prowl, looking to see what's new online, what's changed, what's available. We refer to what their system uses to gather this information as 'bots' or 'spiders' - and what they do as 'indexing' or 'crawling' the web. One goal is to get Google to index your site quickly and to keep coming back, to get it to notice as many pages on your site as possible.

What Sites Does Your Business Need?

Chances are, you've got a website for your business. And chances are, your site's web address is something like: www.YourBusinessName.com.

It's a pretty safe bet your keywords are not part of your business name - although maybe you did name it for your industry and location. That's ok. No matter what your original business website looks like, no matter what domain name you chose, you can always make more.

You may want to invest in some new websites. They'll all lead to you, of course. You'll include your business phone number, your business location, information about your actual business... but these will be sites created around your best keywords. In the industry, we call this getting a strategic domain name.

Simply take your keyword list and go shopping for domain names that feature those words, phrased exactly as they appear on your list. Look for .com domains first because they're still the highest-performing. What happens here is that as people go searching for the products and services you offer in your area, a domain that mimics someone's exact search will do well in the search engine results. Of course you'll need to build websites the search engine likes for this to benefit your business - but you may find your new keyword-rich domain names outperform your original website in no time flat, even with half the effort and content.

What Every Page Needs

Each page on your site will have a different emphasis content-wise, but there are certain technical elements you'll need to work in to have a fully optimized site.

Headline

Every page needs to have a compelling headline that's benefit-driven. Most sites don't have that at all - they'll have some-thing like one of these:

- Welcome to Our Website
- ABC Company Has Been in Business 25 Years
- Forget the Rest, Buy the Best
  (whatever it is they're selling)

Yawn.

Instead, in just a couple of lines, you want to communicate the biggest benefit someone gets from doing business with you rather than anyone else. You probably already know what that is - in business training, they call it your unique selling proposition. One easy way to zero in on this is to identify the biggest pain, fear, or hassle your customers no longer have to deal with because they're doing business with you. People are highly motivated to escape suffering - so if you can show them how they'll do that by dealing with you, you're on the right track.

Not only do you need a compelling headline - it also needs to feature your best keyword. That helps your human visitors know they're in the right place, and helps Google's bots connect the dots and 'get' what your website is about.

Keywords

In the "old days" web developers would just dump every keyword under the sun into your site - even if it wasn't quite relevant, and Google was okay with that. Now, Google has gotten smart, and part of its algorithm involves using something called latent semantic indexing (basically does that language make sense and flow naturally, or does it look like someone went crazy stuffing keywords in where they don't belong, harping on the same words over and over).

Best practice is to have a single keyword (or keyword phrase) you'll focus on for each page. Of course, you'll naturally use other relevant terms in the course of writing your website copy - and that's perfect. But you need to have a single focus for each page.

Your keyword needs to show up in certain places:
- Your headline
- Sub-headlines
- First sentence of the body of your text
- In bullet points
- In your call to action (we'll cover that shortly)
- In your anchor text (we'll cover this, too)
- In your list-building box (coming up, too)

There's a term "keyword density" you'll need to pay attention to, also. Again, in the old days, the rule was the higher the density, the better. Not so anymore. You can calculate keyword density by doing a simple calculation:

- Count how many times you use your keyword in your text.
- Find your total word count for the page.
- Divide your keyword count by your total word count.

The sweet spot is 1-2% density. So, for every 100 words of text, your keyword appears 1-2 times. More than that, and you'll need to be a super-skilled copywriter to make it sound halfway decent. Much more than that, and Google will hate your page and consider it to be spammy (stuffed keywords, garbage, not credible... bad!).

Word Count

Google looks at content length in its evaluation of your web-site. We don't know the magic number for word count, but you'll be in the safe zone if you have a minimum of 350 words per website page. You probably don't want to go over 700 words, mostly because few people will read text that long.

Formatting

People have very short attention spans - especially online. It's pretty rare for someone to read every word on a website page. Instead, visitors skim, scan, and scroll their way through website content, trying to pick out the bits of information they need most.

If you write your content so that it appears as one long block of text, that's a sure way to have your visitors click off of your site and onto your competitor's. Nobody wants to read that way online.

Instead, break your content into short paragraphs. Use sub-headlines and bold them to help move your visitors through your page. Bullet points are a good thing, too - but don't over-do them.

White space is important. Your page should look good, easy to read, welcoming, and user-friendly. Studies show that dark fonts on a light background is the most readable combination. The opposite might look attractive, but it's better to stick with what's proven to be most effective.

Include photos in your website - people always like to 'see' as well as read about how you can help them.

Call to Action

Once you've got a visitor to your website, and they've read your text, what happens next? Not much, unless you tell them what to do. It sounds silly that they won't figure that out on their own, but in most cases you have to actually spell out the next step.

Every page on your website should issue a call to action. Tell your visitors what to do next. This could be having them call you for an appointment, get a free consultation, visit your business, click to get a free report, complete a form, or something else.

Anchor Text

This is a little techy, but it's important. Picture a spider web. There are two main types of web - the pieces that go around in circles, and the pieces that go from the outer edges to the center.

That's a good model for your website. You want to move visitors to your site through your site so they'll get what they need and get into your sales funnel. You also want to create a cohesive site that people can navigate easily.

This is where anchor text comes in. It's a tactic called internal linking. Most of what you'll read about for creating website traffic refers to external linking - also crucial, but different from this.

Anchor text is the words someone actually clicks to get somewhere else online. They're attached to code that takes the visitor to another page or section of your website. Whenever possible, use the primary keyword for the page you're directing visitors to next as the words they actually click on.

For example, on a dentist's website, let's say one page's key-word is "cosmetic dentistry". The text on another page, maybe the Home page, could feature an internal link to a whole new page about cosmetic dentistry that would look like this:

Have questions about <u>cosmetic dentistry</u>?

Visitors would click the words "cosmetic dentistry" and end up on that page.

Here's where a lot of people go wrong if they build their own websites - they'll have people click something like "click here" to move through the website. Do this and you'll entirely miss a great SEO opportunity. Google notices what kinds of words are used in your anchor text, because it further cements its impression of what your site is all about.

Building Your List (AKA Lead Capture)

This topic will be covered more in depth later, but we'll start the discussion here because of how important it is to make sure this appears on every page of your website.

You'll hear online marketers refer to their "list". Here's what that means...

Let's say a prospect lands on your website, reads a bit about your business, even maybe gets excited that they've found you. But then something happens. They get distracted. They go do something else - anything else - besides calling you or following whatever else you've issued as a call to action.

What are the odds they'll remember where they found you?

Not high.

You now have a hot prospect you can't reach. They're gone - probably forever. You certainly can't market to someone who's gone.

If you build a list, you end up with a group of people who want what you're offering, who want to hear from you, who want to do business with you eventually. These will be some hot, self-qualified prospects.

You will need an email service like Aweber or Constant Contact (there are tons more out there, too). These are pretty easy to use, and not very expensive. It's important to use a service like this rather than trying to send hundreds of emails from your own email account. That's a good way to get your account closed. These services specialize in getting your emails out while complying with all the regulations connected to email marketing.

With these services, you'll set up a list, create a form, and get a bit of code to add to your website to make a subscription box. This is just a little area of your site where you'll offer something (usually a free report, a video, something like that) to people who provide their name and email address. For best results, make sure this subscription box shows up on every page on your website. People often don't take action the first time they see something - but if it's on all of your pages, they may join your list - and then you can stay in contact with them until they ask you to stop.

Contact Information

Your business' phone number should be prominent on your page - in your header is an ideal spot. Don't make your site visitors hunt for it. Same thing with your business address if your business is one where your customers come to you.

Credibility Bits

Remember that your visitors have a single question running through their minds as they visit your site - is this business the one I've been looking for? Nobody wants to business with someone who's shady, someone they're not sure is a good solution, someone other people have had bad experiences with in the past.

You can help your perceived credibility by adding the following to your website:

- Your picture - or a picture of your team if you have one
- Logos from associations or groups you belong to (any-thing from your industry or your local business community)
- Logos from any product lines you carry
- Testimonials or reviews from your happy customers
- Logos for the payment methods you accept

What Pages Does Your Site Need?

At a minimum, you need:

Home page

About page

Services page

Contact page

Articles page

Privacy page

Your Home Page

This is the first page visitors will see. It may be the trickiest to get right, because you've only got about three seconds to convince your visitor that they're in the right place to find what they're looking for, that you are the one they want to do business with. It's also likely to be the first page that Google notices.

Your About Page

This is a very important page for establishing your expertise and credibility. On this page, you want to communicate why you're qualified to deliver on the promises you make in your unique selling proposition. Remember, people like to do business with people they know, like, and trust. This page, more than any other is your opportunity to make that happen for your visitors.

Your Services Page

This page is often overlooked because the content may seem too obvious to you as the business owner. For example, if you're a dentist, you know you do dental exams, cleanings, fill cavities, treat gum disease, and do root canals, crowns, partials, and all the other usual dental services. However, you need to spell this out on your services page. It's a great opportunity to highlight anything special about how you deliver these services, too. This page is especially important for showing Google what you do.

Your Contact Page

Even with your phone number displayed prominently on your website, you still need to have a Contact page. On that page, include your address, phone, even a map to your location. Do NOT include your email address there because you're guaranteed to get swamped with a million spam emails then. Instead, you can include a contact form your visitors can complete to contact you.

Your Articles Page

OK, this one's really a blog, but many people have a wrong impression of what that means. This is not the "here's what I ate for breakfast" kind of blog. It's really just an easy way to publish frequently, building the credibility and size of your website while you build a connection with your prospective and current customers.

Having a blog or articles page on your site is so important that we'll give it the whole next chapter.

Blogging for a Boost

Your blog is pretty much a Google magnet if you do it the right way. With a great blog, some marketers get more traffic than their counter-parts who pay for traffic with those sponsored ads in Google. Blogs are updated frequently, which means Google's bots come back frequently - this further cements Google's impression of your website as being an authority in your industry.

Of course, if you do it wrong, nothing good will come from it.

So, let's dig into how to blog well. If you master this for your business, you'll have a huge head start over your competitors.

What Is a Blog?

There are lots of ways to build a website - but one of the most powerful is to have it built using the WordPress blog platform. Google loves sites built this way. Your site will still look like a 'normal' website - but it'll also feature a quick and easy way to publish blog posts (articles, really!). So, you'll have the usual pages for your website, and then also an articles page which features all of your blog posts. You can categorize them, add 'tags' which help visitors find posts that give them the information they're looking for at the time, you can add images, you can even allow for discussion on the content.

Who Needs a Blog?

You.

OK, a little longer explanation. Every business needs to have a blog. It's that important.

What's Involved in Blogging?

Blogs are a lot like articles. (We'll cover articles in the next chapter.) They're more fun to write, though, because unlike writing articles to publish in article directories (again, wait for the next chapter!), you've got complete editorial control. You can write like you speak, talk about whatever you want as often as you want, any way you want. You can be opinionated, somewhat promotional, controversial - however you want to cover your topic, it's all good.

Some particulars:

- Your posts can vary wildly in length, but generally you want to go 300-500 words.

- You'll need a good, compelling title that'll spark your visitors' curiosity and make them eager to read what you wrote.

- You'll also need to write a 1-2 sentence teaser - kind of a cross between a summary and a mini sales piece giving a visitor a reason to read the post.

- You'll need to have a keyword for each post and use it in your title, teaser, first sentence, as an ALT tag for any image you use, to tag your post, and possibly as a category for your post.

- Remember to write using short paragraphs, headlines, subheads, bullets, and white space.

- Always have a call to action at the end of your blog post. What do you want readers to do next?

- You can also create internal links to other blog posts and sections of your website that are relevant to the topic. Be sure to use a keyword as the anchor text.

How Often Do I Need to Blog?

You may not like the answer. Every day would be ideal. No way do you have time to do that, though. So, 3-5 times a week would be really good. Once a week is okay. Once a month is better than nothing.

The neat thing is that with most blog setups, you can write a bunch of blog posts at once and then set them to publish whenever you want them to. So you could write an entire week's worth or a month's worth of posts and then set the publishing date in the future at whatever interval you want. That way you can kind of set it and forget it - and still get all the benefits.

Whatever frequency you choose, it's important to be consistent. Don't be overly ambitious and think you'll blog every day - unless you really get into it, you won't. Most businesses can handle blogging three times a week. The reason consistency is important is that your blog is a great way to train Google to come back and check for new content - and at the same time, you can give your readers an idea of how frequently they should come back expecting new content.

What Should I Blog About?

You'll like this - there are some very easy ways to get ideas. If you think about the prospect of writing 3-5 times a week for your blog from now on, it's more than a little over-whelming. How many ideas could you possibly get for topics to write on?

One way to get ideas is to visit sites where people ask questions about your topic. Yahoo Answers is a great example. You can search on something relevant to your industry and most likely you'll see hundreds of questions asked and answered by real people.

Compile a list of these questions, and keep checking back, and you'll have a pretty-near never ending list of topics to cover. Keep the ideas in question form, because it's always easier to answer a question than to just write off the top of your head. Plus, if someone enters that question into Google (it happens all the time!), your post has a great shot at coming up in the search engine results.

Another way to get ideas is ask yourself some questions about different services, ideas, products, and practices within your industry and blog the answers:

- What is it?
- Why is it important?
- What benefit is there to doing/buying this?
- What if I don't take action?

- How do I do it?

- What if I do it wrong?

- Who could do this for me?

- How often does it need doing?

- How can I learn how to do it right?

- Where can readers find resources or tools that would help?

Yet another way to get an endless stream of ideas is to set Google Alerts for your topic. You'll need a Google account for this (it's free). All you have to do is Google "Google Alerts" and you'll come to a page that walks you through the process. You'll just enter different terms (your keywords are a great start!) you want Google to watch for you. You'll provide an email address where the Alerts will go - and you can specify whether you want to get them daily, weekly, or immediately when Google finds them. You can see anytime that keyword appears in the news, on a website, or in someone's blog. Then just go through your inbox and look for Alerts that spark ideas for your blog.

One thing you never want to do, though, is to copy someone else's article or blog post into your blog. Google has ways of knowing who published it first - and you won't get credit for the post at all if Google thinks you copied rather than writing it yourself. In some cases, businesses have done this hundreds of times a day - the end result was a Google smack that landed their sites useless.

Most business owners find they just don't have the time to write their own blog posts. It's probably one of the most-outsourced projects out there. There are websites out there where you can find a ghostwriter - many online marketing professionals offer blogging to their clients as well.

If you decide you do want to tackle blogging for your business, there are also many courses and books available that can teach you other tips, tricks, and tactics for using your blog to make money in addition to your regular income stream from your business. There are bloggers out there who make very good money just from their blogs.

This should be enough to get you started, though.

Now that we've covered all the basics you need for making your website powerful and effective - and helping Google to fall in love with it - it's time to look at the other half of the equation: off-site SEO.

Make the Rest of the Internet Vote for Your Site

Once your website's in good shape, SEO-friendly, and built for power, you need to start carving out your place in the Internet. It's all about links: creating as many high-quality links on high-quality sites as possible... all pointing to your site as an authority. We refer to all this "pointing" as backlinks.

In the early days, there was a push for begging, borrowing, and buying links from other sites. Google caught on.

Lately, the trend has been to follow the throw a bunch of spaghetti on the wall and see if it sticks model. Google caught on.

Turns out the best way to get links is the old-fashioned way... to earn them.

It does get a little overwhelming here - so get ready, and re-member you don't have to do all of this yourself - or to do it all at once. Online marketers often have tools and other resources that help to make these tasks much easier - so they actually get done! The learning curve and price tag on some of these re-sources are steep, so they may not make sense for most business owners to get for themselves, though.

The general principle behind all you'll need to do to promote your site all over the Internet is that you want to be known in all the right places, constantly growing the perception of your site as being an authority in your industry.

If you think of it, on a massive scale, there are sites you con-sider authority sites - sites where you know for sure you'll get the information, products, or services you need. For example, for books, you'd go to Amazon. For music, iTunes. For an online auction, eBay. For info on medical symptoms or conditions, WebMD. For info on pretty much anything else, Wikipedia or About.com.

Not that these sites are the best, or have 100% accurate information or the lowest prices - it's just that they've built their online presence to the point where they're pretty much unavoidable online.

This, on a smaller scale, is the goal for you with your off-site SEO work. You want it to be that when a prospect does a search on your keywords, you show up all over the place - the clear and obvious leader and expert.

Now, if you had to rely on other website owners to notice your site, like it, want to help promote you, and actually do something about it, you'd be sunk. It'll never happen.

The good news is all of the tasks we're about to cover are fully within your control. You're at nobody's mercy, really. It's a LOT of work to do it all, but it can be done.

Ready?

Submission to Search Engines

Even though we talk pretty much exclusively about Google, there are hundreds of other search engines. Most of them have tiny user bases compared with Google, but there are some diehards who still prefer to use them. We won't even list them here, because most of them are about an inch away from extinction. However, you can do a quick Google search and find them.

Most of these search engines have a tab somewhere that allows you to submit your site. Some of them have a review process your site will have to go through before it's approved. Some of them require you to categorize your site, and to provide information about your business.

You can Google "submit website to search engines" and you'll find links you can use to submit your site. Be sure to submit it to the big three: Google, Bing, and Yahoo. But also submit it to everything else you can find, as long as it's not a search engine dedicated to a topic that's completely irrelevant to your industry.

You'll need to do this periodically. It's tedious. It's pretty labor intensive without tools. But it's important, and if you do it frequently enough, it'll become a pretty straightforward process.

Submission to Local Listings

The bigger search engines now have local listing opportunities as well, and you'll need to get into those listings. We'll cover Google's local listings in a later chapter, but for now, just know you'll need to do that - and to get into every other local listing you can.

An easy way to get started with that is to Google: local business listings. You'll find a long list of places to submit your website.

Again, you'll need to have some key information - details about your business offerings, contact information, keywords, etc. It's really important to be consistent as you create these listings - down to any abbreviations in your address (Street vs. St.). Your listings need to be absolutely uniform in their details. Some of these listings will require a confirmation process where you'll either need to take a phone call or receive a postcard with a confirmation code.

Submitting your business to these listing sites can take weeks to complete. Not a fun process, but again, with practice you'll get faster at it, and it's really important.

Submission to Directories
Search engines are typically automated, so inclusion's pretty much guaranteed if you submit your website correctly. Directories are different. There are human editors there, and your submission will be scrutinized before it's accepted. There are directories for nearly every kind of business or topic under the sun.

You can find directories relevant to your business with a Google search for: (whatever your business is) directories.

You can also do a search for: business directories. This will give you a long list of directories where you can submit your site.

You'll need the same basic information you used for submitting to search engines and business listings. Again, make sure you're consistent with the information you provide in your submission.

Article Marketing
This task is a lot more interesting than directory submission! Because you're an expert in your field, writing articles is probably going to be fairly easy for you. There are guide-lines you'll want to follow to make sure your articles are effective, though. With that in mind, here's a little primer on getting the most out of article marketing.

Article marketing serves two primary purposes for your business. First, it's a great way to build high quality back-links to your website. Remember, Google's looking for indicators that your site is an authority, that it's relevant to your keywords, that other sites respect your site enough to link to it.

If you know enough about a topic to write an article, that's a good sign. If you go to all the trouble to submit your article to respected article directories online, that's a good sign. If your article gets re-published by other websites, that's a good sign. If you get a bunch of readers reading your article, that's also good.

Contrast that with spammers, who throw up a quick website, fill it with garbage text, and stuff keywords into it and you'll see why Google likes articles. There's a saying in the industry that "content is king". If you think about it, only an expert could write an endless number of articles about their topic, and write them in a way that makes sense and provides value to their readers.

So, article marketing is a great way to make Google like your site. But it's also a good way to win human admirers, too. Think about a problem you've ever faced. If you did a Google search on that problem and landed on an article written by someone who truly understood the problem, gave helpful advice, and all along seemed credible, you'd be really glad to have found them. You'd consider them an expert and be far more willing to do business with them than some stranger who simply ran an online ad. In fact, you'd even come to the point of feeling like you knew, liked, and trusted this person - especially if they gave away valuable tips and information that helped you.

This is what we're after with your article marketing campaign.

Who Should Write Your Articles?

Either you or someone you trust to do a good job. Your articles may be the first impression someone gets of your business. They don't need to be prize-winning pieces of literature, but you certainly don't want them to be full of grammatical or logical problems.

For sure you want to either learn how to write effective articles yourself or else outsource this task to a pro. If you're concerned about getting the right information or perspective into your articles if you're not personally writing them, there's an easy solution for this.

If you're working with a ghostwriter and want to be sure they come from the right perspective as they write for you, you can provide examples of other articles you approve. It's as easy as emailing links to articles you like, or you could even set up a bookmarking account (for example, delicious.com) where you can tag articles you like and make that list available to your writer.

Another way you can guide a ghostwriter is to provide audios they can work from to create articles that are in alignment with your perspective. You can either record yourself with a voice recorder or use a recording phone line and provide the link to the audio to your writer. It's much faster and easier to speak about your topic than to write it, and in most cases you could provide enough source information for a good article in just a few minutes.

What's Involved in Article Marketing?

Whoever does the writing, there are certain guidelines you'll want to follow to do this right:

- Your articles MUST be 100% original. Google will find out if you copy someone else's writing, and this will not go well for you.

- Your article should be between 400-700 words. If it's shorter, the major article directories will reject it. If it's much longer, nobody will want to read it; you'd be better off chopping it into two separate articles.

- Your article should be written the way people peak. Never use a big word when a small word will do. Re-member that people's attention span is very short online - and their willingness to 'work' to read your article is pretty much non-existent.

  Make it easy for them to read. In fact, you want to write at about a 5th-8th grade reading level for best results.

- You'll need a compelling title, a teaser (1-2 sentence summary that compels a reader to choose your article to read, even if it appears in a long list of other articles they could choose), the body of the article, and a resource box (this is a few sentences at the end of the article that features your website URL and gives some reason for a reader to click through to your site).

- Make sure you format your article in a way that encourages people to read it. No long blocks of text - short paragraphs, bullet points, and white space are important.

- Use one of your keywords for each article. The keyword should appear early in the title, in the teaser, in the first sentence, in any subheads, in your resource box, and in your anchor text in the resource box. You want to aim for about 1-2% keyword density in your article.

Writing your article is not enough. You need to submit it online to get any benefits from article marketing. We'll cover how you'll do that next.

What Is Article Submission?

There are thousands of article directories online. Some of them are huge - others are tiny. These are collections of articles on nearly any topic. Some of them accept articles on any topic - others are focused only on a single topic.

Most of them make money by having ads - in most cases they get a small payment anytime someone clicks the ads. By growing the directory and becoming known for having quality content, these sites can become very lucrative for their owners. Their business model only works if they can load up on articles people actually want to read.

These directories are frequented by people seeking information, and by website owners who want to re-publish articles rather than creating their own content. In that case, the articles are free to the website owner as long as the article is republished in its original form, complete with its resource box intact. It's a system that works well for everyone involved.

Some of these directories are automated and accept every article that's submitted. Others have stringent guidelines and human editors who must review and approve every article they publish. Google especially likes that kind of directory because there's almost no chance a garbage article will get published.

For most of these directories, you'll need to create an account for your business. Some allow you to just paste your article into a submission box - but most want you to create an account and submit that way. The better directories have a probationary period where your articles are heavily scrutinized before they're approved. With those, you'll be limited as to how many articles you can submit at a time until you've been vetted.

In a nutshell, what happens when you submit your articles to directories is that you cast a vote for your site being an authority on behalf of those directories. You create a backlink each time your article is published online, in each of those directories. Google takes notice!

The submission process isn't much fun. It's repetitive, boring, and often full of snags. You'll find it's anything but guaranteed your article will be accepted. You've got to learn and follow the guidelines for each of the major sites at least, to have a chance of having your article published. Some of the most frequent problems that could get your article rejected include:

- It's coming up as being 'duplicate content' meaning too much of your wording is too similar to something else that's been published online.
- It's too promotional. You can be promotional in blog posts on your site, but not in articles. The editors just want valuable, useful information - not a sales pitch.
- The keyword density is too high. If your keyword appears with more than 2% frequency, some of the

directories will reject your article or ask you to rewrite it.

- If you've got objectionable content, or content that otherwise violates the authors guidelines, it'll be rejected.
- If you try to include links in the body of your article, it'll be rejected. Links (usually a maximum of two) are usually acceptable in the resource box of your article - but in the better directories, they can't appear in the body.

While there are thousands of article directories out there, you can get some good results even just by submitting your article to a few of the best ones. In many cases, your article will get republished in many places because a website owner found your article in that directory. At a bare minimum, you'll want to submit your article to EzineArticles.com, currently the most-respected article directory out there.

How Many Articles Do You Need?

Article marketing should be a regular part of your marketing campaign. The more you do, the better - as long as you follow the guidelines above to create high-quality articles. Ten articles a month would be enough to make a powerful impact fairly quickly. One a month would be way more than most business owners do on a regular basis. It depends on your resources.

What Should You Write About?

Whether you write for yourself or outsource this task, you'll need to come up with a list of topics to cover. Your keyword list is a great place to start. You can use your list and the topic discovery methods listed in the section on blogging to come up with some great ideas.

There are two types of articles that are proven to be a hit with readers and publishers: Top 10 lists and how-to articles. The reason the list type article is so popular is that a reader's chances of finding valuable information that scratches their particular itch is multiplied by how many points are in the list. The how-to article is a reader favorite because it's actionable and pretty much guaranteed to feature good content.

If you check out an article directory like EzineArticles.com, you can see what kinds of articles are most-read and most republished. Use what you learn to create articles that are likely to be well-received like that.

Press Releases

Press releases are one of the most powerful ways to build your online presence. Google LOVES them. By nature, they're high-quality content (just the facts - no promotion), and in most cases are reviewed and approved by a human editor.

Most business owners completely ignore press releases as part of their marketing strategy because they don't think they've got news to share, they're still stuck in thinking of traditional media, and they don't know how to do a good press release.

As far as having news to share, pretty much anything going on in your business can be turned into a newsworthy event. Do a quick Google search on reasons to send a press release, and you'll find hundreds of happenings your business could use for ideas. It doesn't have to be earth-shattering news - just news.

As far as traditional media goes, the odds of your press re-lease leading to a newspaper article, TV spot, radio interview, or anything even close to that are slim. That's not the point. The point is to get some of the highest quality backlinks available by publishing your press release online. You're not at the mercy of a journalist or print publisher who's got space restraints and needs to sell papers - publishing a press release online is much, much easier. Of course, you can submit your press releases to traditional media outlets and hope for the best - in some cases your story will get picked up. But don't focus on that.

As far as not knowing how to do a good press release, that's easy to fix, too. If you're working with an online marketing firm, they'll handle it for you. If you're not, you can outsource this task to a ghostwriter. The best ones have a simple questionnaire you can complete so they'll have all the information they need to create a great press release for you. And if you want to handle this task on your own, you can find books and courses online to learn all the particulars.

The basics you'll need to know as you write press releases for your business:

- These are news pieces. You can't have salesy language at all - just the facts.
- Make sure you cover the who, what, where, when, why, and how to get a complete story.
- You'll need to use neutral and impersonal language. This is different from your blog posts and articles, where you can be more personable. A press release shouldn't have first- or second-person pronouns in it. The only exception is in the quote segment. You'll want to quote someone: an expert, a company representative, a customer, someone like

that. This quote is the only place in the whole press release that can be slightly promotional, opinionated, or personal. It's also the only part that can include a first- or second- person pronoun.

- You'll need a strong headline that compels someone to read the release.

- Use one of your keywords per press release. It should appear in the headline, the summary, early in the first sentence, and then sprinkled throughout the release where it fits naturally.

- Follow a press release template to be sure you cover all the pieces and parts and have them in the proper order and format.

You'll need to submit your press releases to press release distribution sites in order to get any results. There are dozens that are good and free, and one that's fantastically powerful and rather pricey. That one's PRWeb.com - and you'll need to spend a small fortune per press release (just for distribution - you've got to write it) if you go that route. For many businesses, that's not an issue. For businesses that have an acute public relations problem, it's worth it. A press release distributed through that site will show nearly immediate and totally massive search engine domination.

If you're not in the middle of a crisis or don't have that much allocated for press release marketing, just do a search in Google for press release distribution sites. For some of them, you have to create an account - for others you just upload the release. Obviously the free sites will yield just a tiny fraction of the results you'd get with PRWeb.

Video Marketing

Video is one of the hottest marketing tools online today. Studies show that websites featuring videos get visitors staying longer than if there was just text on that page. Google notices how long your visitors stay, of course, so anything you can do to get them to say longer and visit more of your pages is good.

One reason video marketing is so effective is that Google loves video - in fact it loves video so much it bought YouTube! It's always a good idea to feed Google the kind of content it loves best.

Most business owners think first of TV ad type videos - and those are great, but can be very expensive to create. There are several other types of video you could create for a fraction of the cost. Most of the video creation processes will require some software and a bit of a learning curve. Local online marketing professionals typically have this technology and know-how to create high-quality videos.

Outsourcing this task may be a better use of your resources, but some business owners may want to try it on their own.

Article Videos

Once you've got articles created for your business, you could transform them into videos. There are several ways to do this - one is to paste your content into a PowerPoint presentation, the record the presentation using a screen recording tool like Camtasia. For audio, you could go with nothing, music, or reading the article aloud.

Image Videos

You could also create videos that focus on graphics. Using professional stock photography and little bits of text, you can create some very visually appealing videos. There are a few software programs that make this easy and kind of fun to do. Be sure to use music and images that are approved for commercial use.

Live Action Videos

This is more like a TV ad sort of video. You'll need to have a professional video company help with this, unless you own top-notch video equipment.

What Should You Do with Your Videos?

You should include videos on your website - on the Home page and any other page that could be made more appealing and interactive by adding a video. Your blog can also include videos.

You should also create a channel on YouTube for your business. This will help your prospects and customers to stay focused on your videos rather than finding just one and then ending up watching videos from your competitors, or videos that are completely off-topic. If you have a channel for your business, all of your videos will appear to the side, and your viewers can watch your whole lineup with far less distraction.

Other than on your site, you'll need to distribute your videos just like you do with your articles and press releases. There are a number of syndication tools that help this process, but typically they're out of reach for individual business owners - only an online marketer would have enough projected usage to justify the investment in these.

You can, of course, distribute your videos on your own - it'll just take more hands-on work. Do a Google search for: video sharing sites. Other than YouTube, there are several other video distribution sites you may be able to submit to, depending on your topic and the type of video you've created. Be sure to use your keywords in the title and description of your videos.

Those are the primary types of marketing pieces every business needs to create and distribute online to build high-quality backlinks. In the next chapter, you'll learn how to use Google Places for maximum results.

You May Be Doing THIS Wrong

Google Places (it's had a few different names... but it's those map listings you see when you do a Google search for a local business) is one of the most powerful tools you can use for your business - if you do it right. In fact, as many as 70% of online searches turn out to be for local businesses, products, and services. Google spotted this trend and is leveraging it big-time, featuring local results at the top of search results pages.

These pages are already indexed and in most cases show up on page one. In fact, many business owners who are just learning about this tool are shocked to see their business is in the top spot - and they haven't even completed their profile yet. If you optimize your profile, you'll see your listing's effectiveness skyrocket.

Your Places page will display basic information about your business. If you haven't done anything with it yet, there still may be information there - gathered from the online Yellow Pages and other directories. Just because it's there doesn't mean it's correct information - or that you can't vastly improve the results you'll get by tweaking your page. Here are the basics you need to know about maximizing the power of your Google Places page.

Provide Complete Information
Just by completing your profile, you'll make it easy for your prospects to get the information they need and want about your business. This boosts your odds of them becoming your customers.

Make sure you include the following:
- Hours of operation
- Brands you carry
- Special offers, coupons
- Photos, videos
- Links to your website, blog and social media profiles

Even if you don't do more than that, at least get your page claimed - or someone else may do it! It's sneaky; it's wrong;

it happens all the time. Your competitor may claim your page to keep you from using it!

Once you've claimed your page, there's still a lot more you can do to turn it into a traffic-generation tool that increases your Google prominence dramatically. Here are eight tips for getting the most from your listing:

1. Help your new customers find you easily. Use the exact business name and precise address to describe your business and location.

2. Make it easy for them to call you. Always use a local phone number answered by a real person.

3. Show them your site. List a link (make sure it works!) to your website. Many of your prospects will check out your site before calling you.

4. Categorize your business. Google Places gives you several to choose from. Be as specific as you can - if you find one with your keyword, that's even better.

5. Make your listing irresistible. You'll be able to use your keywords and your unique selling proposition in the "Description and Custom" fields for your business.

6. Let them see you. You can upload photos and videos to add even more credibility to your listing. People love to get as much info as possible about your business before calling, and this adds a bit of a

personal touch and helps them feel like they know, like, and trust you.

7. Don't be shy. Publicize your positive reviews and testimonials by asking your happy customers to leave a review for your business on your Google Places page. This will help get "social proof" working in your favor - people like doing business with businesses people like.

8. Make a deal. You can offer coupons and special deals to visitors to your Google Places listing. This alone is a great way to pull in new customers. Be sure to have them let you know they found the deal on your Google Places page.

Follow this pattern for all of your online business profiles. Keep them updated and optimized to get maximum impact in the search engine results. It takes a bit of time and attention to stay on top of this, but it'll pay off.

Why You Need Positive Reviews

Word of mouth advertising is the hands-down winner for most businesses - online reviews are just as powerful - maybe more. Not only do your prospective customers take these reviews into consideration, so do the top search engines. The more positive reviews you have, the higher your Places page will ultimately go - at least theoretically! Again, nobody knows the algorithms Google uses, and sometimes there are bizarre cases of one business with a ton of great reviews getting ranked lower than a business with no reviews, or even a couple of dings in their record.

Just think of how you search for local businesses to provide a service for you. If your roof is leaking, you'll search for a roofer in your town. Chances are, there will be several who come up in the Places section. Which one are you most likely to call?

About Getting Reviews

You might be shocked to know how many of your prospective customers go looking for reviews about your business before they'll even hit your actual website. They'll read these reviews and then decide whether to look further.

You've got to get into the practice of leveraging positive reviews. We'll get into a discussion of online reputation monitoring in a later chapter, but for now we'll just focus on getting positive reviews for your Google Places page. You can check yours out now, if you've got a Google Places page. You'll see a star system for rating, and a couple of places where Google's practically begging your customers to leave a review.

Getting them to actually do this can be a challenge.

- Some business owners implement a subtle rewards program to encourage their customers to leave reviews. Be very careful if you go this route. Google frowns on 'buying' reviews.

- Some business owners actually pay outright for reviews. There are unscrupulous services worldwide that will sell packages of reviews super-cheap. This is a sure way to get in trouble with Google - most of the reviews are identical, vague enough to work for any type of business, and signed by the same 'users'. Google's way smarter than that, and it's just a matter of time before these businesses get caught.

- Some business owners work with a permission form to collect reviews and login information to handle posting them on behalf of their customers. Also a risky process - and not that likely to work. Would you give your login information to someone?

- One smart way some businesses are meeting this challenge is to invest in a mobile device or iPad they can use at their business to have happy customers leave a review on the spot. They'll provide an info sheet with suggestions for how to write an effective review so it's easy for their customers to do it.

If you ignore this task, you run the risk of making it hard for people to find your business - even if they do know your business name. You'll also leave a bad impression with your prospects because having an incomplete business profile makes it look like maybe your business is out of business.

There are only so many spots in the Places section - typically no more than seven will appear on the first page. Beyond that and someone would have to click a little link that tells Google to show more results on the map. There is no way to pay for a higher placement.

You want to be sure your business is showing up on that map. Especially in larger towns and cities, it's important for your prospects to be able to gauge how close you are to their location. The map makes that possible instantly. While you may lose some prospects who decide you're too far away, chances are you'd have lost them anyway once they figured out where you're located. For others who are close-by, showing up on the map close to them may be the final tipping point to steer them your way.

No denying it - there are a lot of directories and business profiles out there to manage. The task can seem over-whelming because you've already got so much on your plate. This may be a good task to hand off to an online marketing expert so you can just focus on doing what you need to do to keep your business running.

In the next chapter, we'll dive into online reputation monitoring - even from this quick overview of Google Places, you can see that never before has it been more important to know what people are saying about your business online.

They Said WHAT About Your Business?

With the Internet's power, it's never been more important to know what people are saying about you and your business. Someone can leave negative reviews about your business in forums, blogs, articles, press releases, websites or Google Places, and do major damage to your business before you even know what happened.

Take a guess what happens when a prospective customer reads negative reviews about your business - especially if they're prominently displayed at the top of Google's results... Click! They go to your competitor's site instead. The one with the good reviews.

You can't ignore what's being said about your business. It will either help you or hurt you. Either way, you've got to know so you can help yourself.

What Is Online Reputation Monitoring?

Online reputation monitoring helps to monitor and guard your online presence. It makes it possible for you to know right away when people say anything - good or bad - about your business. That makes it possible to do damage control if it's bad, or leverage positive press if it's good.

Horror stories abound about businesses that were targeted by irate customers or even malicious competitors who used the Internet to pretty nearly destroy businesses they didn't like. It's crazy, but not unheard of for people like this to build entire websites dedicated to slamming a business they decided to target. Sometimes they'll even go to great expense to publicize their discontent. In some cases, they even hijack an unclaimed Google Places page to wreak havoc. That's bad enough, but if you don't even know it's happening, you have no chance of protecting yourself.

How Can You Protect Yourself?

There are two elements to an effective online reputation management strategy. One is monitoring what's being said, and the other is building a hedge of protection for yourself.

Monitoring What's Being Said

There are a number of ways to monitor what people are saying about you online. One of the easiest ways to get at least a rough monitoring system in place is to set Google Alerts for your name and your business' name. This will allow you to get an email every time Google notices you're mentioned. As soon as you get one of these alerts, be sure to check it out and see whether it's positive, negative, or irrelevant. Unless you've got a very unusual name, you'll get a lot of alerts that refer to someone else.

If you get a positive alert, consider how you could use the contents to further improve your Internet presence. Maybe you could link to it from your social media accounts or include it in a blog post. In some cases, you may even be able to use the content in a press release, if it's newsworthy enough.

If you get an alert about a negative mention, you'll want to address it as quickly as possible. The appropriate response will really depend on the nature of the complaint - but you'll want to do whatever you can to fix it if it's justified, or bury it if it's not.

If you find yourself in the situation of needing to bury unjustified bad press, you're actually in reputation repair mode now. One of the fastest ways to bury bad search engine results is to displace them with positive ones that the search engines trust. There's no faster way to achieve that than to invest in a press release with PRWeb. It's costly, of course, but in some cases a press release distributed through that service will show up fairly quickly and dominate pages of search engine results. It's not a permanent fix, because as the press release ages, it becomes less powerful - but it will give you time to create other online content to help your cause.

The Hedge

OK, remember how search engines work? You type in a search term and get a list of results. Nobody's likely to go past page one unless they're really motivated to do thorough research. One way you can build a hedge of protection for yourself online is to own your own name search results. If you can lock up the whole first page or two of search results for your name and your business name, you'll make it harder for someone to blast you online.

You build the hedge first of all by making sure you own do-mains featuring your name and your business name. While the variations here are endless, with .com, .net, .info, .tv, .co, .org, etc. (depending on your country) you may want to invest in several for added protection. This can be gradual. What you're doing is preventing someone else from buying a domain featuring your name.

Reputation protection is another reason to be sure you've claimed the Google Places page for your business.

You also want to be sure you create content (articles, press releases, and videos) that use your name or your business name as a keyword. They will show up and take up valuable real estate on that front page of Google, making it more challenging for someone with malicious intent to break into those top spots.

The key to online reputation monitoring, management, and repair if it comes to that is having a system that lets you stay vigilant in protecting yourself. It's not a task most business owners have on their radar - or know how to do efficiently, but it's important.

In the next chapter, you'll discover one of the best ways to stay in contact with your customers while helping your business to grow exponentially.

Reach Your Customers On the Go

If your customer base is anything like the majority of the population, you can pretty much rely on one fact: they are completely addicted to their mobile devices. This presents a great marketing opportunity and another way your marketing can crash and burn – all in the same little gadget. You've probably heard of mobile marketing. There are a couple of meanings for that term, and we'll cover them both.

The first 'mobile marketing' is text messaging, or SMS for short. With mobile text messaging, you've got a powerful way of reaching your customers and prospects anytime you like. It's almost a guarantee... if you get a text message, you'll read it. Right now there's no more effective way of getting your customers to pay attention to you, especially if you make it worth their while to read your texts and take action.

Mobile marketing is one of the most effective ways you can communicate with your customers today. It won't stay that way forever, because technology is always bringing the next new thing - but for right now (and probably the next few years) this is a tool you need to consider for your business.

Here's why:
- More than 90% of adults in the U.S. own a mobile phone.
- More than 95% of all text messages get opened.
- More than 90% of those messages get opened within less than an hour.

Print, email, and other forms of advertising and promotion don't come anywhere close to the read of mobile marketing. People just don't pay attention to any other form of communication as much as they do to texts.

What Kind of Text Messages Should You Send?

Depending on what kind of business you have, there are lots of possibilities. Here are just a handful:

- Restaurants might offer a buy one get one free, free dessert, kids eat free, free appetizer, or something else to entice customers in on slow days.
- Offer a rainy day (or other weather-related) special to stir up business on what might have otherwise been a bad revenue day.
- Offer a deal to your customers who bring a friend in.
- If you have an appointment-based business, you can text reminders so you don't have no-shows. Offer a special if you see a last minute hole in your schedule.
- Use holidays - the more creative the better - to offer your customers a deal.

You'll need to keep your messages brief so they don't get cut off. You'll also need to experiment a bit to see how frequently your customers want to hear from you. Once a week is acceptable to most customers - but what's appropriate for your business depends on what type of business you have.

How Do You Do This?

You will need to have access to a text message marketing service for this to be manageable. It's not really a tactic you can do on your own without a messaging platform; unless you don't mind sending out just ten messages or so at a time to your entire interested customer base, gathering their mobile numbers and entering them into your phone manually, and being sure to delete any who ask to be removed from your list.

A good platform will allow for your customers to sign them-selves up to receive your messages, then let you send them all at once. Typically the customer sign-up process involves posting a sign at your business offering your customers a deal for registering on the spot. They'll text a certain message to that platform in order to register - and then you'll have their mobile number and permission to send them special promotions until they ask you to stop. If that happens and you're using a mobile platform, they'll be removed from the list automatically.

This is one of those marketing methods that's worth trying out - even if you personally hate the idea of getting promotional messages on your phone. If you make it worth your customers' while to get these messages, they will like getting them. They can always unsubscribe if they get tired of hearing from you; and there are ways to make sure that doesn't happen. If you offer something of value (information, discounts, or freebies) in every text you send, your customers will read your messages almost every time.

Text messaging may not be appropriate for every business - although the applications for different business types are growing all the time. But it's worth taking a look at to see whether it'll work for yours.

The "Other" Mobile Marketing

When you hear marketers talking about mobile marketing, they may be talking about text messaging – or they might be talking about mobile-friendly websites. It won't take long to figure out which they mean if you listen for a little while.

What Is a Mobile-Friendly Website?

The percentage of searches people do online on their mobile devices rather than on a laptop or desktop computer is skyrocketing. We're a society that's always on the go, so this makes sense. Many predict the number of searches done on mobile devices will soon greatly outnumber searches on home computers. This means you need to know how to make your business accessible online for your customers and prospects who search for you on the fly.

You're out running errands, traveling, sitting in a meeting, waiting for your kids, or any of a million other scenarios where you're away from home – and you need to find a business that offers a certain product or service. Do you wait until you're home to search online for it? Not if you have a smart phone or other web-enabled device. Your customers and prospects are the same – they may be looking for you online using their mobiles.

This is great news – if your site is mobile-friendly. Mobile sites load quickly and are easy to navigate even on the tiniest of touch screens. You know from your own experience searching online using your mobile – if a site won't load quickly enough, you move onto the next site. If the navigation on a site is complicated and slow, or requires you to complete boxes with your information, you'll bounce to a site that's easier to use.

In addition to making your navigation easy and intuitive, you need to pay attention to the priority of information you're providing. Because your mobile searchers are usually in a hurry, it's even more important that what they find on your site first meets their needs and grabs their attention so they'll stay on your site long enough to determine that your business is exactly what they need.

Does Your Site Work on Mobiles?

It gets a little technical here, but to make sure your site works properly on a mobile, you'll need to make sure it's coded correctly. In some cases, all you need to do is install a plug-in that automatically determines whether a visitor is using a mobile device or regular computer to get to your site, then adjusts how the site performs. If your site was built using a platform that doesn't work with plug-ins, the coding involved is a bit more complicated and not something you'd want to try to do on your own.

No matter who built your site, and how they built it, you can check your site's performance on your own phone – then ask your friends, family, and employees to check on their mobiles as well so you can see how it shows up on different devices.

Ever See a QR Code?

You probably have – and may not have known what you were seeing. QR codes (or Quick Response codes) are a handy marketing tool that works with mobile devices. They're little square graphics you can scan with your smartphone to get a deal or some other kind of special or information. They were originally used for storing information about car parts – but are now used for marketing.

QR codes appear in newspapers, drive-by signs, in email marketing, text messages, and posters. Some business owners even have a QR code printed on the backs of their business cards. The technology allows marketers to collect and store valuable information about your customers' interests and preference and to run analyses that will prove useful for your marketing campaigns.

Contests and coupons are some of the most successful uses of QR codes. Uses that are engaging and valuable are most likely to get your customers sharing them with their contacts, the ideal outcome.

Getting a QR code made for your business is a bit involved, but you can do it yourself with some research and technical skills. If you're working with an online marketing firm, they'll be able to help you with this as well as helping you track the performance of your codes.

In the next chapter, we'll take a closer look at email marketing. Is this a strategy that still works? Should your business use it?

Can You Beat the Delete Button?

Used to be that email marketing was THE surefire way to build a list of prospects and customers, stay in touch with them, and market to them. Now some marketers are finding that customers' physical mail boxes are more fruitful ground for marketing than their email inboxes. Is email marketing still a good use of your resources? And if so, how can you get the best possible results?

You can blame it all on overload.

Way, way back in the day, getting an email was kind of exciting. The novelty wore off a long time ago, and now most people consider their email boxes a necessary evil, a mix of messages we can't wait to read and those we'd just as soon delete without ever opening. The joke now is that your email box will still be full after you die, so don't even bother trying to empty it.

If you consider the messages your spam filter ensures you never even see, you probably get hit with literally hundreds of emails every single day. How many do you open, read, and take action on?

Very few.

If you're going to use email marketing - and it's still a valuable tool for most businesses - you have to figure out how to do it so your messages get read and acted on rather than just deleted or marked as spam.

First, yes, most likely your business needs to be doing email marketing. We covered this a bit earlier, but the primary reason is that building a list of people who want to hear from you means building a valuable asset. People who find your website and are interested in what you offer, but for whatever reason don't buy right away will be lost to you forever unless they join your list, giving you permission to contact them.

Even with its drop in effectiveness, email marketing remains an affordable tool that can get you good results if you do it right. The biggest reason it still works is that the people who subscribe to your list are at least somewhat interested in what you offer.

There's a fine line between effective e-mail marketing and spam, though. If you email too often, or don't give your readers a valuable reason to read, you'll annoy them and instead of them being eager to learn more or do business with you, you'll leave them wanting nothing to do with you.

Again with the fine line, but if you email too infrequently, you'll have the opposite problem. People who were once interested in your business will forget who you are or why they were interested in the first place.

Balance is important. You need to have balance in your frequency of emailing and the mix of promotional and informational content. If every message you send is an advertisement, your readers will unsubscribe in droves. A good mix some marketers find is about 25% promotional and 75% informational.

Now, on to some particulars about how to do this right.

Make the Subject Line Count.
Mess this up, and nobody will read your emails. The subject line is a lot like the headline on a newspaper. It needs to be

clear and catchy, but not hype-filled or misleading. Walk this fine line or risk aggravating your readers.

Avoid Long, Wordy Messages.

People are too busy to read paragraph after endless paragraph. Write your emails so they're easy to skim, scan, and scroll through. Subheads and bullets help with this.

Include a Call to Action.

Decide what you want your reader to do next. Do you want them to buy something? Click something? Download something? Call you? Come into your location? They won't automatically do it; you have to tell them, and give them a reason to do it. Don't give them a long list of actions to take - make it simple... ask them to do ONE thing.

Identify Yourself.

We read left to right - and that holds true in our email boxes as well. There are a lot of decisions being made in a fraction of a second when someone gets your email. We tend to open emails only if we recognize the sender and trust that reading their message will be worth our time and attention. The "from" field of an email may be even more important than the subject line now - especially for your existing customers.

Be sure to include your contact information in plain sight within your email message as well. Include: phone numbers, website address, and your business' physical address.

Get Someone Else to Write for You.
Writing may not be your strength - or the best use of your time. Many business owners hire ghostwriters to create their email messages for them. It's worth the investment to have well-written, professional emails reaching your customers and prospects.

Edit, Proofread and Do It Again.
If you decide to write your own messages, remember that spelling errors and incorrect grammar can land your messages right in the trash bin. Make sure your content is perfect and professional.

There's a lot that goes into a success email marketing strategy - and you can learn more by taking a course or reading up on the topic online. Many business owners decide to hand off this task to a marketing partner rather than spending the time and energy involved in doing it effectively.

In the next chapter, you'll learn how to tap into the world of social media profitably for your business.

Get Social and Make More Money

Love them or hate them, the worlds of Facebook, Twitter, LinkedIn and the whole rest of the social side of the Internet represent money in the bank for the business owner who uses them right.

Ignore social media at your own peril - use it wrong and you may as well throw money through a shredder; but do it right, and you'll position your business in a sweet spot where you can connect with your prospects and turn them into lifelong customers who can't stop raving about your business.

Not sure social media's all it's cracked up to be for local business marketing? Google and Bing have both revealed they weigh social media into their local search results. They don't reveal anything about how this information figures into their algorithms of course, but just knowing they're looking makes it worthwhile to work with a social media campaign if you want to dominate the search engines for your market. Could mean the difference between a top ranking and slipping onto page two or lower.

Why Should You Bother?

What works is always changing. Traditional methods of marketing lose their effectiveness, or come back into power - you never know what'll happen next, what will be the next best way to reach your target market. Right now, social media is one of the most affordable and profitable ways to get new customers into your business. These prospects are online - and social media is one of the easiest ways to reach them right there.

Social media is the closest relative to word-of-mouth advertising available to you as a business owner. It's a great way to get near-instant credibility, even loyalty, with current and new customers while you attract new ones. People flock to these sites to get information and to connect with others - and they don't just do it now and then; most people check into their accounts multiple times a day.

Create a social media plan, build an effective presence on these sites, post relevant content, and see how easy it is to cement your position as an expert in your industry. While branding is just part of the picture, you'll find it's easy to subtly create brand awareness among your followers and friends online. This is because with these sites, you can relate to your ideal customers meaningfully and regularly. By paying attention to their updates, you can also gather valuable market research pretty easily.

Lots of business owners wonder how they'll know whether their social media campaigns are actually working. The best way to measure your results is to gauge how much people interact with your profiles – and ultimately, of course, whether you see an uptick in new customers coming into your business. Do they "like" and "follow" and re-post your comments and updates? Do they post positive reviews and testimonials on your page? Link to your profile from theirs?

Setting Up Your Profiles
You'll want to set up a business profile - even if you have a personal profile - on Facebook and Twitter at a minimum. LinkedIn may be helpful to you as well. Make sure your profile is as complete as possible and that you've used your keywords where appropriate.

Don't believe for a minute that any one social media site is enough - no matter how much you like or hate a particular site, there are millions of users who prefer one or the other and use it regularly. Ignoring either could mean leaving lots of business on the table.

Privacy is not your friend on these sites when it comes to marketing your business. While you might want your personal profile to be accessible only to people you know, your business profile needs to be public. This will help your search engine ranking, where a private page will do nothing to help you move up in the search results.

The Name of the Game Is Being Liked... A Lot
Liked, followed, connected - it all comes down to people finding value in being associated with you in social media. The more popular your business is among the users of these sites, the wider your reach.

Getting people to connect with you can take some finesse. Don't beg people to "like" or "follow" you on social media - give them a reason to want to do it. Discounts on your products or services, free gifts, and valuable information remain prime incentives.

Make it easy for people on your mobile marketing or email marketing list to connect with you via social media. Include your Twitter, Facebook, and LinkedIn info and a special offer for those who connect there. This is a great way to put your prior marketing efforts to use another way.

Consider using Facebook advertising to build your fan base. If you do it right, it's cost-effective and you can target your prospects very narrowly. You can make it so your ad only shows up for users from certain demographics, geographical areas, or with specific interests.

Who Should You Hang Out With?

Be on the lookout for businesses that are complimentary to yours, targeting the same ideal customer you're looking for - then see how you could connect with these business owners and help them. If you work together, you can find ways to grow both businesses as you better serve your customer base.

Bing in particular seems to pay attention to your fans and followers as well as who you're following. This makes it worthwhile to seek out prominent businesses with lots of followers and connect with them.

What Should You Post?

Stay relevant and fresh. Put some thought into what you post - don't just do the same old thing all the time. You can do some quick research to find out what people are interested in related to your industry - then write your updates from your perspective on these popular topics.

Preserve your positioning as an expert by guarding your con-tent. If it's junk, don't post it. If it's going to throw your business' professional image into question, don't post it. Never post if you don't have anything valuable to post. There's always something you can post that will add value to your followers - even if it takes a little bit of digging and thinking to come up with it.

You can leverage your work by linking your social media sites, or at least using the same posts and updates across the board among the sites. Chances are you'll have different followers on each of the social media sites - at least in part. Beyond that, both Google and Bing say links posted on both Facebook and Twitter weigh into their algorithms.

Your competitors are using social media - that's pretty much guaranteed. No matter how you feel about these sites, you can't afford not to use them. It can seem overwhelming at first - and it is a big task to stay on top of your social media campaign. But it will pay off for you in building more and better connections online with your prospects and existing customers if you'll dedicate the resources you need to do it right.

Seems like a lot of tasks to juggle, doesn't it? In the next chapter, you'll learn how to keep all of this online marketing going throughout the year without letting anything slip through the cracks.

Nothing Gets Past You

It all comes back to having a plan. Marketing your local business effectively online won't just happen. It's a big job, one you can't just leave to chance or do when you get around to it.

There's no way you'll be able to stay on top of all the tasks involved in online marketing without a marketing calendar. You've got enough to do just running your business without trying to save space in your brain for remembering when you'll do what for promotion. Before you know it, holidays creep up on you and marketing opportunities are lost because you somehow didn't see them coming or just didn't have the resources needed to reach out to your prospects and customers.

Every one of the tactics and strategies in this book needs to be done on a regular basis for best results. There's just no getting around it - either you need to do this for your business, or you need to outsource this battery of tasks so it actually gets done.

Here's how the professionals handle it: they use a marketing calendar. This could be as simple as creating a spreadsheet with an area for each month and each tactic, then a plan to follow. A marketing calendar makes it easy to keep track of what's coming next, what's actually been done, how much it cost, and how it worked for your business.

Using a marketing calendar also makes it easy to capitalize on events and holidays throughout the year. You can do a quick search online to find a list of holidays - everything from the usual holidays you already know about to some that are strange, funny, creative, controversial, or obscure. Every single month there's something you could use to tie into your business, connect with your prospects and customers, and create revenue.

It can take a while to find the ideal mix for your business. How many articles, press releases, videos, and blog posts do you need each month? How many social media updates per week? What should you text or email to your customers?

But rather than waiting until you magically guess correctly at the answers to these questions for your business, you'll do better to get started. The sweet spot for your particular business may take some time to discover - but you won't find it by speculating. And most likely it won't stay the same for long. As new tactics arise, you'll need to work out how to incorporate them into your online marketing plan, too.

Having a marketing calendar spreadsheet makes it easy to track your results so you can do more of what's working best for you, and begin to understand what might be going wrong on tactics that aren't producing the results you want. You'll have to really keep your eye on all of this if you're doing it yourself so that you don't waste even a minute of your very limited time. Even if you end up working with an online marketing firm, you'll want to keep tabs on your results.

Some metrics you'll find important to look at monthly at a minimum:

- Website traffic. What really counts is unique visitors. You'll find a lot of other counts, like hits and pages, but what you really care most about is how many different people visit your site.
- Website dominance. An online marketer has tools that report how your site is ranking for a whole host of key-words, but you can do some poking around

in Google to see how you're doing for some of your top keywords. Just do a search using your keywords and see where you come up.

- How are your new customers finding you? Make it a practice to ask them so you'll know which strategies are paying off best for you.

Keep an eye on your return on marketing investment. Very few business owners have any idea how much it costs them to get a new customer, or even how much that new customer will be worth to them in the coming year. These are valuable figures to know because they will help you make better decisions about your marketing. Almost every business owner has run a marketing campaign that went into the red - but to do it again and again because you're not aware of your results is a sure way to end up closing your doors.

In the end, marketing your local business online is a huge job. It's not one you can ignore. The Internet's not going anywhere anytime soon. Overwhelming? Possibly. But it's also an opportunity to reach your market like you've never had before. Compared with traditional forms of advertising, you can reach exponentially more prospects for the same money. It's all about having - and following - a solid plan.

Hopefully this book has given you a clearer understanding of what you need to do to promote your business online effectively. If you decide you'd like some help so you can focus on running your business instead of all the tasks involved in marketing it online, let me know. We can take a close look at how your business is doing online now, what's needed to improve your online presence, and how to reach your goals together.

Glossary

Above the Fold

Just like on a newspaper at a newsstand, you can only see part without flipping the paper over. On a website, this is the part that's visible without scrolling.

Affiliate

Someone who promotes your products and services and gets paid based on results.

Algorithm

How search engines create a list of search results based on the search term. Algorithms change regularly to yield better search results.

ALT Text

Coding that tells the search engines about images and other non-textual elements that can't be displayed.

Analytics

Graphs and charts that provide information on your website's traffic and the source and behavior of your site's visitors.

Anchor Text

Words, phrases, or images that are 'clickable' – when you click, you are taken to another part of the website or elsewhere on the Internet.

B2B

Business to Business marketing

B2C

Business to Consumer marketing

Backlinks

Links coming into your website from another place online. Backlinks help with SEO because some algorithms calculate the quantity and quality of backlinks when determining search engine result ranking.

Below the Fold

Any part of a webpage you have to scroll down to see.

Black Hat SEO

Search engine optimization that uses unethical methods.

Blog

An online journal or article page that is updated frequently, usually allows comments.

Bots

Short for the robots (also called spiders) that scan the Internet for search engines.

Bounce

When a visitor reaches your website and leaves it quickly without visiting any other pages on your site.

Bounce Rate

The percentage of your site visitors that bounce.

Browser

An application that enables you to access and navigate the Internet.

Code

Information written in any of several computer languages.

Competing Pages

The total of webpages that are focused on a single keyword.

Conversion Rate

The percentage of how many clicks to your site generate a sale or a lead.

Crawl

An automated process where search engine algorithms gather information about websites.

Deep Linking

Linking to a page on your website other than your Home Page.

Description Tag

An HTML (code) tag that provides a description of the page for search engine listings.

Directory

An index of websites, usually created by human editors. Usually require editorial approval for inclusion.

Directory Optimization

Writing a directory submission in a way that makes it most relevant for search engines to increase the chances of the site coming up when someone searches with your keywords.

Domain

A text Internet address ending in a dot and three letters (i.e. .com, .net., .org, etc.). In countries outside the U.S. domain names end with a two letter country code.

Duplicate Content

Webpages that have the same content – can be on a single website or on different websites.

Ecommerce

Buying and selling products and services online.

Flame

Comments or messages posted with the intention of being rude or abusive.

Geo Targeting

Adding geographical information to marketing campaigns to make the marketing pieces more likely to appear to searchers in that location.

Google Dance

Each time Google changes its algorithms, Internet marketers scramble to understand the impact of that change and then make any adjustments needed to their online marketing.

Google Sandbox

For various reasons – from having a brand new site to employing Black Hat SEO tactics – sometimes Google essentially shuns a website, and it basically disappears from search engine results.

Google Smack

Getting your site put into the Google Sandbox.

Googlebot

See bot.

Hidden Text

Text added to a webpage that is the same color as the page's background, making it invisible to humans. Search engines can read the text. This is a Black Hat SEO tactic.

Home Page

The main page of a website, its main point of entry.

Hyperlink

A bit of text or an image you can click on a webpage that takes you somewhere else, either on that page or to another page or another website.

Inbound Link

Any link that comes into your site from another website.

Keyword

What someone types in when they search for information online. Can be a single word or a phrase.

Keyword Density

How many times a keyword appears on a page for every 100 words.

Keyword Research

Research done to determine how people are searching online for the information, products, and services you offer.

Keyword Stuffing (or Keyword Spam)

Trying to include too many repetitions of a keyword in an article or website content in an effort to trick search engines into giving higher importance to the website. This is a Black Hat SEO tactic.

Keywords Tag

A list of relevant keywords for a website, entered into the coding of the site. Early on, the search engines paid attention to the keywords tag – now most ignore it completely, as its abuse was an easy Black Hat SEO tactic.

Landing Page

The page on a website where you land after clicking through a link on another website – either from an affiliate's page, an article, press release, or video. It is designed to get a visitor to take action.

Link Building

An SEO practice with the goal of boosting a website's traffic and improving its ranking in the search engines. Links can be created with articles, press releases, videos, blog posts, etc.

Link Checker

An automated tool that helps identify broken hyperlinks on a website.

Link Popularity

How many sites link to your site, and how well-respected by the search engines those sites are.

List

An email marketing list comprised of site visitors who provided their name and email address, willingly giving you permission to market to and contact them.

Long Tail

Keyword phrases 2-5 words long. They get fewer searchers, but they are more targeted and often yield better conversion rates.

Manual Submission

Building backlinks by hand rather than by using an automated tool.

Meta Tags

Bits of code that provide information to search engines about a website. They include Title Tags, Description Tags, and Keyword Tags.

Navigation

How you move from page to page in a website.

Organic Search Listings

Listings in a search engine that are not sponsored, or purchased, as an advertisement.

Outbound Link

A link that leads to a website that's not your site.

Page Rank

Search engines use algorithms to determine the relevance of a website, then list them in order of relevance.

Podcasts

Audios and videos that can be distributed online, down-loaded, and played on a personal computer or mobile device.

PPC (Pay Per Click)

Paid placement in a search engine. Your ads only show up when someone enters the keywords you bid on for your ad. You only pay when someone clicks your ad.

Reciprocal Links

Links exchanged between website owners.

RSS (Real Simple Syndication)

A way to syndicate your blog content online so it reaches subscribers automatically every time you update the content.

Search Engine

A program that scours the Internet in the attempt to match searches and web pages.

SEO (Search Engine Optimization)

Working on a website to make sure it is found easily by people using targeted keywords to search for information, products, and services online.

Search Engine Submission
Submitting URLs to search engines to make the engine aware of their existence.

SERP (Search Engine Results Page)
The results you see after doing a search in a search engine. The SERP includes sponsored ads and organic search listings in a list.

Social Media
Various websites that feature user-contributed content, including social networking sites, forums, blogs, video sharing sites, and more.

Title Tag
An HTML tag coded to create the text that shows up in the top line of a browser when you visit a website. Also used by search engines to help them provide relevant search results.

Top Ten
The top ten websites appearing in the organic search listings on a SERP.

Unique Visitor
An actual, real visitor to your website. Unique visitor stats don't include bots or repeat visitors, so this is an important statistic to measure.

URL

The Internet location of a webpage. Follows the format http://www.domain.com (or other domain endings).

Web Directory

An organized, categorized listing of websites, sometimes centered around a specific topic.

About the Author

Heatherr Jumah is a business and marketing strategist specializing in working with entrepreneurs and small business owners committed to being high-value, in-demand celebrity experts in their fields. Heatherr is the expert people turn to when they're ready to leverage the Internet to its full potential and step into the spotlight with a powerful online presence.

Using innovative branding, marketing, and publicity strategies, Heatherr helps her clients increase their visibility and get more recognition so they attract a steady stream of high paying clients.

Through her seminars, teleclasses, and consulting practice Heatherr has been working 'behind the scenes' with small business owners across the world since 2007. Having run and managed businesses for over 21 years Heatherr is able to provide her clients expertise and knowledge based on real world business experience.

Here is my contact information:

Heatherr Jumah
Heatherr Jumah International
www.CreatingFameOnline.com
Info@CreatingFameOnline.com